SITTING AT EYE LEVEL:

My Life as an Advocate, a Professional, a Woman, a Mom and a Person with a Significant Disability

SANTA PEREZ

Copyright © 2018 Santa Perez

All rights reserved. No part(s) of this book may be reproduced, distributed or transmitted in any form, or by any means, or stored in a database or retrieval systems without prior expressed written permission of the author of this book.

ISBN: 978-1-5356-1404-7

Dedication

I am dedicating this book to my Mom, Estela Q. Perez. My mom has been the soul of my existence, the backbone of my life. It would have been so easy for my mom to listen to the doctors and put me in an institution and forget about me, but she did not. My mom taught me everything I know: never give up, always love your family and take care of your kids. My mom taught me what being a woman really means.

Mom, I never will forget the stories you told me when you were a kid, the nursery songs that you sung to me over and over and over, the dirty jokes that you told me just to make me laugh, the unwavering faith in God, which kept me from doing evil, and the unconditional love that you taught me. Thank you Mom, for letting me *fly*, when you were afraid for me. You have been the best Mom I could ever have. I know I am the best Mom I can be to Noah, because I had the best.

Contents

Introduction 1
Santa Elia Perez 3
My Childhood 9
The Wooden Chair (and Bell) 19
Dad 21
Stella (Ek-ah), Rosie (Oh-ee) and Tony (Huero) 25
My Education 29
With Two Dits and a Da 35
The Men Come, The Men Go 39
One Hundred and One Ways to Heat A Burrito 53
The Story of Noah 57
Raising Noah 65
Becoming An Advocate 73
An "X" Does Not Mark the Spot 81
Dear Un-Typical Child 85

Introduction

My name is Santa Elia Perez. I was born in East Los Angeles, California. I am 55 years old, a Hispanic woman and I have Athetoid Cerebral Palsy (CP). My CP is severe. I cannot feed myself, dress myself, or bathe myself. I also have a severe speech disability. Only my family and close friends can really understand me and, with a lot of patience and understanding, I get my point across. I was considered to be non-verbal, which is so ironic, because anyone who knows me can testify how non non-verbal I am. I am a nationally recognized leader in disability rights.

I tell you this now, because in spite of my severe CP, I have had an extraordinary life. I have had so many great, wild, crazy, happy, and sad experiences that many other people might not have had disability or not.

My hope for the reader of my book is that they look at disabilities in a different way, a fresh way. My hope is that you see all people for who they are and not only for their disability.

So often we see people with developmental disabilities and intellectual disabilities and have preconceived notions about how their lives are supposed to be, and we forget about their humanity.

I am not a hero, nor do I want to be. I want to be a good role model for other people with disabilities, so they are inspired to live their lives as they want.

This book has been a long time in coming. Many people throughout my life have asked me to write this book, but I never thought that my life was really interesting. I have never attempted to write a book before, so I'm winging it. Well, here goes. I always thought that a book or biography went from the beginning to the end (well one part of an end), but now I have learned, that doesn't have to be the case. I learned that you can emphasize different parts of life that were important or interesting or those that have amended my life.

There have been SO many people that have guided me throughout my life and have made me the woman I am today, Santa Perez. Some of these people I have thanked over and over, but for some, I have never thanked. For everyone, I am writing this book for you!

Santa Elia Perez

(Opening scene) *(on the back steps of my house on Cleon Avenue, Sun Valley, CA, my abuelita (grandmother) is singing "Cielito Lindo" and she is telling me to sing with her as she sings.)*

I WAS BORN IN Los Angeles, California. My mom and dad were immigrants from Torreon, Mexico. Actually, my dad was born in Los Angeles, California, but he was raised in Torreon. My father, Anthony C. Perez, was in the Army when he met my mother, Estela Quimiro, in Los Angeles, in the 50's. He was just about finished with his tour in the Army when, while being on leave and taking a drive in Los Angeles, he saw my Mom walking on the street and he pulled over and started talking to her. My Mom said he had a nice car. Soon thereafter, they gotten married and started to have a family. First came Stella, my oldest sister, then came Rosie, my other sister and then they had Tony, my brother. My dad had always wanted boys ever since they got married and began having children.

So, after the third child, they decided to try for another boy, to have a matched set. Maybe that was a mistake.

On August 27th, 1962, I was born. The doctor was not too worried about my mom, since she had had three previous pregnancies without any complications.

Mom started to get contractions on a Sunday after church. Dad had stayed with her for 24 hours, and then he decided to go home since I was going to take my time. It took ten more hours for my mom to have me. It was hard labor. The doctor never thought about performing a C-section. They said that they were not prepared. Anyway, I was not coming out because I was turned the wrong way, breech, and the doctors had to deliver me via forceps. When I finally came out, I wasn't breathing and did not breathe on my own for seven minutes. There was mayhem in that delivery room. The doctors kept on coming and going; talking to each other and saying that they did not like my color of my skin. They had to give me oxygen. After stabilizing me, they took me to the neonatal intensive care unit (NICU) and put me in an incubator. I could only imagine what my mom was thinking. At that time, my mom was a young immigrant woman who barely knew English. She had just wanted to give birth to her "son," who would be named Art.

Meanwhile, in the NICU, I was not doing so well. Apparently, I had stopped breathing again, this time for 20 minutes. If the first time wasn't bad enough, this time the lack of oxygen would cause me to have brain damage, which would result in cerebral palsy (CP).

Someone had called my dad to come back to the hospital. When he came, he brought my abuelita with him. They probably were expecting to come see the newest addition to the family, a pink little girl.

My mom told dad that the doctors wanted to talk to him. She said "I think there is something wrong with the baby." The doctors had stated that the lack of oxygen would result in some degree of brain damage; their prognosis was that I may not be able to talk, hear, or walk, may be mentally retarded or even die. Anticipating the worst, dad and my Niño (Godfather) had decided to baptize me in the hospital, just in case.

Mom went home from the hospital, but I had to stay for another week. The doctors advised my parents to put me away in an institution and forget about me. That was the typical pre-rehearsed script in those days…if something is wrong with your child, forget them and start over

Thank God my parents said "No, when can we take her home?" My mother was (and still is) a very wise woman. Before my parents brought me home, mom gathered my two sisters and my brother in the bathroom, (somehow all of our important family meetings were held in the bathroom) and explained what had happened. I'm not really sure if she understood herself. After answering what I am sure were a million questions, mom asked them what they would do. The answer was a choice - they could put me in an institution or bring me home. It was unanimous. I was coming home.

I don't know if I had been given a vote, that I would have said yes. After all, the Perez family was about to go through the most dramatic and life-changing event of their lives. For that matter, so was the whole Quimiro family.

In most Hispanic families, there is more than just the immediate family. There are tias and tios (aunts and uncles), ninas and ninos (Godparents), grandparents and cousins, and lots of family. I had them all!

Normally, when a family gets a new baby, it's a big adjustment, but when a family gets a child with a disability, it can be devastating. I don't think my family had ever heard the word "disability" prior to this. Even having a child with a disability in the family was unheard of. How will they ever adjust? For my parents and siblings, they were about to step into a whole new world full of new vocabulary, services, evaluations, doctors, therapies, new hardware, and so much more.

My abuelita was the head of the Quimiro family. She was a strong little old lady with a tough disposition. My abuelita's name was Santos Quimiro. She was very stern with her children and grandchildren. She had four daughters and two sons, but none of her children had named their children after her. So, when my mom got pregnant, she promised her that if I was a girl, I would be named after her, hence Santa. Santa means saint, a name that does not quite fit me, just ask anybody who really knows me.

My Childhood

WE LIVED IN A LITTLE two bedroom house at the top of a hill in Los Angeles. The house was small and it had an even smaller house in the back. A line of steep concrete steps led up to the house and it had a big front yard.

When I came home, I was like any other baby. Even with everything that had happened at the hospital; I seemed to have come out of it without any obvious issues.

Abuelita did not trust doctors too much, so when mom told her that "little Santita may be sick," she said that the doctors were crazy. She told mom that the doctors did not know everything and they were only making everyone worry over nothing. But still, Abuelita was a little hesitant to let my sisters and brother hold me. She told everybody that they had to be careful with me. I was special. (Ah. Now isn't that special!!!! Can't you tell that I was going to be one of her favorites?)

I had green eyes; something that my dad proudly claimed was from his side of the family. Only my brother and I have light colored eyes.

When my mom took me for my first doctor's visit, the doctor examined me and he told her that I looked fine; that there was nothing wrong with me. Maybe Abuelita was right after all. But something was wrong. I was not reaching the typical developmental milestones. After three months, my mom noticed that I had trouble sucking the bottle. She found it easier to feed me with a little spoon and I had a hard time holding up my head. I was not sitting up at the age I should have. Also, my hands were always clenching (especially the left hand). It was hard for my family to understand; they knew something was wrong, but they did not know what it was.

At the second doctor's visit, the doctors noticed that some things were not right. My eyes were crossed and I would later have three surgeries throughout my childhood to correct this. The doctor thought that I was too fat. He scolded mom for feeding me too much and told her to put me on a diet.

After reducing my diet, mom then noticed that I was different. My tongue would stick out and I started drooling even before I started teething. Mom regretted listening to the doctor.

My first year was full of going to see doctors, therapists and hospitals for observation and tests. I still was not doing the developmental things that I was supposed to do. The prognosis was that I had CP. The doctor had reassured my mom, that I would grow out of it by the time I was six years old… (I'm still waiting to grow out it). To add to all the fun, I also developed asthma! This condition would become one of my least favorite as it has been a constant annoyance in my life.

I was non-communicative and I was lethargic. I did not show any emotion until one day as I sat in our car. This is how my mom explained it:

We were in the car, coming back from yet another doctor's appointment. She looked at me and wondered if I was really "there." So she told me something funny (it was probably a dirty joke, my mom is notorious for telling dirty jokes). I guess she wanted some kind of reassurance for herself, that she did the right thing by keeping me. Anyway, I started laughing hysterically, something that I had never done before. That's when I finally "clicked" into my life. Mom started laughing and crying. It was like she knew that I knew who she was and I knew who I was too.

That was the beginning of the bond that my mom and I have. It's a strong, unchangeable, unconditional, intense bond that most mothers and daughters will never have, but we were lucky in that way.

When my mom had Rosie, my middle sister, mom developed asthma, which got worse after I was born. The doctor had suggested to my parents to move to a dryer climate for her health and now mine. So, dad and mom bought a two-bedroom house in Sun Valley, California. That two-bedroom house eventually turned into a three-bedroom house, which turned into five-bedroom house thanks to my dad's ingenious carpentry.

I was going to Children's Hospital of Los Angeles for therapy. That is where my Mom and I met Mrs. Garby. Mrs. Garby was the psychologist and she was the first advocate for me. Mrs. Garby was good for my Mom. She knew what services I needed and how to get through the red tape. She knew the system and was able to teach my mom the tricks of the trade.

Mrs. Garby told my mom to put me in day care at Rancho Los Amigos. I don't remember much about it, except for three vital things that happened to me. First, it was far away. I remember spending a very long time (what I thought was hours and hours) sitting in the car just to get there. It was a pretty big place and outside it had a big playground. The most memorable place for me was the pool; this pool was in this impressive, nice, sizeable building. I think it was an Olympic size pool, but then again, anything is enormous to a three-year old. I remembered that pool, because I almost drowned in it.

One day, we were in the pool (the wading pool yet) and I slipped through the inner tube that was four times my size.

No one saw me sinking into the water. I could see everyone splashing and playing around me from under the water, but nobody could see me. I couldn't get myself back up. Finally, someone saw me and pulled me back up. That is how I developed my fear of water. I love to take baths and go swimming, but I need to know that someone is watching me at all times, still to this day.

The second thing that was important was I met a lady named Karen. Karen had CP like me. (Although no one has the same level of CP, everyone's severity is different.) Her facial muscles moved involuntary like mine did. She was a teacher, a member of the staff, someone who was independent, and she could even drive a car. Karen was the first woman that had a predominate disability who was just living a typical life, someone who I could look up to, my first role model.

When she held me up in the pool, I could feel all her tightened bony fingers hold me up. She squeezed tightly and it kind of hurt and I wondered as she was holding me, who was holding her?

The most important experience at Rancho was when I met Susy. Susy was a little girl with sandy brown hair and a very squeaky voice. Her left hand was very spastic and she could not use it. She was always smiling and laughing. She was a year younger than me, but when we met, that was it. We became best friends instantly. Susy and I had a lot in common. We both had about the same level of CP, although her speech was much clearer than mine. We both were the youngest of our families. We both were Virgos, which meant that we thought alike. And we both had parents who did not really like each other. We developed a camaraderie that would last us throughout our lives. Our friendship has lasted over 50 years.

We were always hanging out together. We went through elementary school together and had some extraordinary experiences. We were known to some as the "Bobbsey Twins" on our angelic days, while others referred to us as "Tweedle-dee and Tweedle-dum" in our scandalous days. We would often be seen on the school playground planning our next great adventure, i.e., sleep overs, trips to the mall, going on trips; taxi cab rides….you name it.

I think, since we couldn't play like the typical kids, we had to invent our own fun and we did. Our play was more of verbal play and imagination, but we always had fun.

The greatest thing was we were going to start school and we found out that we were going to go to the same school: Charles Leroy Lowman School. Lowman was a school for physically disabled children. In those days, the word "mainstreaming" did not exist.

I was always jealous of my siblings when they went to school. They always got new clothes, school supplies, and brand new metal lunch boxes. Now it was my turn. I guess I was anxious and excited, because I could not sleep that night, thinking of what a big girl I was, going off to school.

There were a lot of kids with many different disabilities. Some walked with crutches, some had walkers, some had braces on their legs, some had big wheelchairs, and there were some kids who did not look like they had anything wrong with them at all.

The doctors and therapists had determined that I needed braces on my legs, so that my legs would grow nice and straight. I guess they thought at some point I would be able to walk.

Mrs. Sherry was my pre-school teacher. Her room was filled with all kinds of toys, colored paper and there were pictures on the walls. There were two classrooms connected by a big bathroom in the middle and outside was a patio with swings that had seat belts on them.

Lowman was a regular academically-geared school. They taught us everything other typical kids learned in school, except that we had additional learning facilities. There was a physical therapy department, an occupational therapy department, a speech room, and a pool.

If you asked "What was the best part about Lowman?", we would have to say it was the teachers. For the first time in our lives, we were only known as students. Yes, everyone had a disability, but the teachers' main goal for all of us was to teach us academics. Even though we had to learn how to adapt to our physical limitations, we still had to learn reading, writing, and arithmetic.

There is always that one special teacher, the one who saw you for you and was never afraid to push you to your limits. For me, that was Randy Benson. Mr. Benson was my P.E. teacher at Lowman. When I first met him, I fell in love with him. But so did everyone else. He had brown hair and blue eyes. I think the great thing about him was his sense of humor. If you were ever depressed or angry, you could always count on him to cheer you up.

He was also the swimming teacher at Lowman. The previous PE teacher wasn't as nice as Mr. Benson. The old teacher would ridicule you and yell at you if you didn't do something right. He made me afraid of the pool. So, when Mr. Benson came along, the pool was not my favorite place. One day Mr. Benson said we were going swimming and said "let's try the water wings." Water wings are a type of swimming device. I said, "No way." He said. "Oh yeah, we'll see." Well, I tried the water wings and now that's the only way I swim. He always had a way of making me do things when I was afraid to. Mr. Benson knew that I was hesitant to go back in the pool, until he gently persuaded me. The first day he said "Ok Santa, you don't have to go in, just come and watch us have fun.", and I did. The next time he said. "Hey Santa, why don't put your swim suit on and put your feet in and splash them around, that's it.", and

I did. By the time Mr. Benson was through, I loved going in the pool again. P.E. was fun again! Mr. Benson liked to try new things to make games and stuff more accessible to his students. I was always his guinea pig, which was fine with me. I got to get out of class and spend time with my favorite teacher.

As the years went by, Mr. Benson was now Randy and I developed a meaningful relationship and that childhood crush turned into a respect for him. Randy became my foster dad. Now, Randy never knew this. I have had a lot of friends, but nobody could be like Randy. To this day, we still keep in touch, calling, sending holiday cards and seeing each other whenever we can.

The Wooden Chair (and Bell)

Back in the day, when I went to grade school, the buses didn't have wheelchair lifts. Every morning around 6:30 a.m., Mom would have me ready with my lunchbox to go to school. The sound of the big yellow bus billowed down the street and we went outside to greet it. The driver would say, "Good morning," as he lifted me onto the bus and sat me on a seat. I think there were seatbelts, but I'm not sure. My Mom would stand on the sidewalk, waving as we rumbled down the street to pick up the next kid. There were several stops whining towards Lowman.

At school, there was a little wooden chair waiting for me. It was small, with wheels on the bottom and two cutout handles in the back for somebody to push. It had two cutout circles on both sides. I don't know what the cutouts were for, maybe just for décor?

At that time, I was considered to be non-verbal. I did talk, but no one could understand me, except for my family.

The teachers and aides needed to know if I needed or wanted something, especially if I needed to go to the bathroom. So, they tied a bell to one of the holes on the chair. This was the first piece of assistive technology that I learned. The aide said "Santa, if you need to go to the bathroom, ring the bell." So, I did.

Back in the day, wheelchairs only came in four styles: adult wheelchairs, gray or green; or child wheelchairs, gray or green. I was six when I got my first green wheelchair. It was shinny and new and I could use it at home.

Dad

My Dad was a good man. Everyone who knew him loved him. He would help anybody if they were in need, but to his family, it was a different story. He was very stern and raised his kids with an iron fist, literally. Dad was not the touchy-feely type. We had to steal affection from him, every chance we got and I only heard "I love you, Mija" one time in my life and that was because I made him say it. I think this is why my siblings and I tell our kids that we love them all the time. I know, at least for me, that I always want Noah to know how much I love him, even when I'm gone.

My Dad was a carpenter by trade and he knew how to create things from nothing. Growing up, he would create things that would make my life easier and more accessible. I presumed this was his way of showing me that he loved me. The most memorable creation was the BIG checker board. At that time, learning motor skills was important, so Dad got this huge piece of wood, cut it to a big square and made a checker board. He drilled out holes and painted the squares red and black. For the markers, he used wooden dowels, half were black and half were red. This way I could put the dowels in the perspective holes to play checkers and get some physical therapy in my hands. Another time, we were at this novelty gift shop and we saw this BIG light switch. Dad installed it in my room, and afterwards, he moved my light switch lower to the floor so that I could reach it when I sat on the floor.

Like I said, he ruled with an iron hand, but in my entire life with him, he never physically abused me. I guess he felt guilty for my disability. Now, for my two sisters and brother, that was a different story. I always felt bad about that. I guess "parenting" was different back then.

Dad taught me about money and how important it was. One day, he sat me at the table with a pile of money on one side and a stack of bills on the other side. He said, "See all this money?" Then he got a bill and put the correct amount of money on top. He said you need to pay your bills before anything else. You need to take care of your money at all times. Even though he had a good job, he was tight with his money.

The best times were when we were with family; at an amusement park or camping at Yosemite National Park, or a back yard barbecue. He would play cook and he had the knack to put the right amount of lighter fluid so that you could taste it as you took a bite of meat.

My dad was a weekend alcoholic. Now, I know that some people are going to get mad and dispute this, but this is my truth and this is my book. It took me 30 years after he died to admit this to myself and to say it out loud. If you think I've got Daddy Issues, yes, you're right and I can admit that.

That was the biggest issue that my Mom and Dad had in their marriage…my Dad's drinking. Dad was a beer man and he loved his Coors beer. He would go to the bar Friday night and wouldn't come home until Sunday morning.

Now, I'm not saying he didn't take care of his family, because he did. Every Thursday was pay day. He would stop at the corner store and buy the following: one mango for Mom, a newspaper, the newest edition of the TV Guide, a gallon of orange drink for us, and, of course, a six pack of Coors Beer. He would park on the couch after dinner and watch what he wanted to watch on TV. Mom and I would have to beg him to watch want we wanted, *I Love Lucy*.

Dad had his silly side too. He loved the oldies, Chuck Berry especially. He would dance my mom around the living room and we would laugh and laugh. He would say that we were the three musketeers and for a long time, we were.

The saddest part of this story is that he always told his daughters how much he wanted grandsons. He only got to meet three of his grandsons out of ten grandsons and four granddaughters in our family today. It's sad to me because he has awesome grandkids, but his mistress Coors stole him away from us. My dad was 52 when he died.

Stella (Ek-ah), Rosie (Oh-ee) and Tony (Huero)

When I was a child, I couldn't pronounce my sibling's names, so I did the best that I could. Their nick names are still around, even today. I have been blessed with three awesome siblings. They have been my role models all of my life, even though they did not realize what they were voting for when my Mom had asked them, "Should she come home from the hospital?"

Being the youngest always comes with jealousy and having a significant disability couldn't have helped at all. I know I took an enormous amount of my Mom's time. There wasn't enough time in the day to parent everyone and care for me. I think my Mom did the best that she could on what skills she had, but still, my siblings suffered.

I always felt bad for them when they couldn't do something or go somewhere because someone had to stay home to watch me. I sometimes felt I was an embarrassment to them and they would hide me away so their friends wouldn't see me. Kids will be kids I guess.

My sister Stella was the oldest. She got to do everything first. Stella loved me no matter what. The fondest memory I have is the time we went to Knott's Berry Farm. She was waiting in line to get on a ride. I was sitting on the side, looking through the fence, wishing that I could ride. When Stella got to the front of the line, she looked at me. When it was her turn, she ran, picked me up and we rode the ride together. Stella has become one of my best friends. I can tell her anything. When she got married, she made me her Maid of Honor.

My sister Rosie and I have not had the greatest relationship. There has been some resentment over my Mom. My fondest memory of Rosie is the clothes line experience. Somehow I think that if she showed me how to walk, I would walk. Her ingenious plan was to strap me up to a clothesline and make me walk. Did it work? Of course not, but she gets an A for trying! I love the times I spent with Rosie. They are few and far between, but we always had fun and a good laugh.

Tony, my brother, is a great man, even though in our childhood, our sibling rivalry was bad. It wasn't until he left for the Air Force that I saw the beauty in him, and we became great friends. Tony taught me about love and sticking with it, even when his other half wasn't that deserving of his love. I admire the fact that he raised his kids as a single dad for many years after his wife left him.

Tony was the catalyst for making me move to Las Vegas. It took me many years to finally say yes, but when I did, he welcomed me with open arms.

We never really talk about the effects that siblings have when one has a significant disability. How do they approach the topic when they meet a potential partner? Is it a conversation of great inclusion or is it of great despair? I don't know the answer.

Today, I can report, we are all great friends and I can rely on them just as much as they rely on me. They have given me lots of nieces and nephews. I love how my nieces and nephews love and respect me. They don't see my disability at all; they only see me as the cool tia (aunt) and Nina (Godmother).

My Education

As I mentioned before, I went to a segregated school from elementary to junior high. I remember learning about history from a little orange book and the teachers lecturing us from the front of the room, just like any other school in America. We had tests every Friday in what we had learned that week. To my notion, we were learning our lessons like everybody else, except when one of us students would be pulled out of class for therapy or speech or something else. This would happen once or twice a day. Sure, therapy was important. This is where we learned about our life skills and how to be independent: walking, climbing stairs and learning to dress ourselves. I still put on my jacket the way they taught me. Put your two arms first, then swirl it around your back, then let it slide down your back, However, there would be a price that would be paid. This infraction would be with me for the rest of my life.

In 6th grade we were being taught the multiplication tables. Mrs. Zucker would pull out a 45 RPM record and would play it over and over until we learned that numbers times table. It was very effective and fun. I learned my times table up to 6. However, on the week we were going to learn #7, I was pulled out out of class. I think some visiting therapists came to learn some new techniques and they needed a guinea pig and that guinea pig was usually me. Nevertheless, when I got back to class, they were already at #10. I lost 7, 8, and 9. I still can't do math.

Another big deficit I have is grammar and spelling. By the time you read this book, it will be edited at least three or four times. The problem was all through school, the teachers and aides would write everything down for me. I would only have to dictate to them. I never would have to physically spell out the words; therefore, I never got to learn the skills of writing, actually putting the letters to form words, seeing them on paper and learning the grammar rules. I before E except after C, whatever, you get the idea. Yes, I got good grades for "writing" and "spelling," but, I think, if they really tested me, I would fail.

At Lowman and Miller (Junior high) , the therapists had tried different ways to teach me how to use the typewriter. They tried putting my arm in a device that would hold my arm up and I could use one finger and since the other four fingers would get in the way, they tried to bind the other fingers in a sock, with one finger sticking out. That didn't work. The old helmet with a pointer trick didn't work either. My head would bounce around too much. They were running out of options, until I said "I can use my nose." My nose was convenient, nobody had to set me up, hook me in, or take me off. And let's face it, my nose was always there, nobody ever had to put it on, and it was ready any time I needed it, except when I had a cold. Ah-choo! There were some drawbacks with nose typing too. My back and neck started to hurt me a lot and I was not a fast typist.

Miller wasn't equipped to have any type of assistive devices. They just had the old IBM typewriters lined up in a row for the students to use. I had a composition class where we only had to compose one paragraph per day. This was good and bad for me. The good part was I only had to peck on the typewriter an hour and that was the right amount of time before my back started to hurt and it took me that much time to peck out one paragraph anyway. The bad part was I only had to compose one paragraph per day. The low expectations that the teachers had for us would prevent us from being scholars later in life. I do, however, feel the teachers did the best that they could with the knowledge they had. They were only charged with providing six years of our education (good or bad), then their students moved on. This limited education would not prepare me for life at college and beyond.

Miller was a unique school and it was adjacent to a typical high school. Miller's high school students would go across the street to be in typical classes and to be mainstreamed and maybe, just maybe, learn more academically.

I was in the ninth grade and I was excited about the thought of going to that school on the other side of the street. I asked Miss Perrol about my classes. She said "Oh, you're not going next door." I said, "Why not?" I wanted to go to that school and I had the right to go. She said reluctantly, "Ok Santa, let's make a deal, you can take one class and we'll see how well you do." I don't remember what class it was, but I remember it was hard. I was so unprepared to learn in a typical school. There was so much reading, so much writing (for my aide), and so much remembering. I still can see my dad and mom studying with me, so I could learn the class work assigned to me. But somehow I (we) did it. After that first class and the first semester, I ended up taking all my academics and graduated from that school across the street.

That was the start of my becoming an advocate. I was learning to speak up for myself.

I wound up going to a junior college my first four years. I was still academically behind. Writing a term paper seemed like a mountain to climb and I still typed with my nose. I don't know how I did it, but I did. I had lots of help along the way.

My take away is teachers need to have higher expectations for their students. Teachers need to make sure that their students are really learning and learning in their own unique way. Today we have assistive technology to assist students.

Teachers, if you have a kid that you know, "has it," push them! Raise the bar.

Students, if you want something more, go for it! Ask for it! Don't be afraid to have high expectations for yourself, and then have the people around you have the same high expectations for you too!

With Two Dits and a Da

In 1989, I graduated from California State University, Northridge (CSUN), with my bachelor's in Psychology. In my mind, I was ready to "conquer the world." I thought that I had all the skills I needed to be a competitive employee…silly me.

I was volunteering at CSUN in the Office of Disabled Students. An old friend, Gayle Pickering, was an adaptive tech specialist and someone who had known me since I was five. One day, she asked me what I was going to do now. I told her that I was good on the computer and I wanted to find a typing job. She said "You are not ready. You need another way to input into your computer. You are too slow and no one will hire you." It hurt me, but she was right.

I was still typing with my nose as I did in school. I was still having the problems with my back and neck always hurting me and I was not becoming a fast typist. Nevertheless, I was reluctant to try something new. I had grown accustomed to nose typing and accepted the fact that it will always be painful to type. But with a lot of persistence from Gayle, I decided to try something new. After all, I will always have my nose to fall back on! Ouch…

Gayle and I tried many different adaptive devices. There were some good adaptive devices back then, but we needed to find the right one that would fit me. It was so easy to grab the newest technology and make the person fit to that technology. Maybe it was funding, maybe it was trying to keep up with the Joneses, but I wanted something that was easy and that would complement me. I needed this device to be able to work in all applications and occasionally double as a communication device. We tried many different kinds of assistive technology (AT), but the best for me was the Words+ EZ-Keys Morse Code software. After figuring out the best position to place my body so I could work the dual switch, I was a Morse Coding fool! We had decided to use two small switches that would be placed under my chin, so that my head and neck would be straight and comfortable all the time. I had learned Morse code in two weeks. I went from typing 3 to 5 words to 25 words per minutes.

About a month later, I got my first job as a data entry person at United Cerebral Palsy in California.

Sometimes, I use my AT for communication. I know it's easier for people to understand me. I use it when I need to give big presentations and such; however, I much prefer having someone interpret what I say. Maybe if I had gotten the AT earlier in life, I'd have used it more, but I find it cumbersome and time-consuming. I feel I don't type fast enough and I'm making people wait too long. I know this is all in my head.

> *"Friends- Some have known me all my life and some are new. Some have left my life and some have stayed. Some have seen me at my worst and some have seen me at my best. Some have seen my ass, choked me, dropped me, dressed me and bathed me. Some have made me stronger and some has made me weaker. But I know in my heart that ALL of my friends have helped make me who I am today!!!!! I love my friends."*

The Men Come, The Men Go

ALL OF MY LIFE I haven't had good luck with men. I think I am at my best when I'm in a relationship with a guy. Society just doesn't understand anyone with a disability as we are human too. We need affection, love and sex. I am a woman; I need affection, love and sex.

A lot of guys don't even look at me in a sexual way. I'm always in the "friend zone." have a philosophy on this which I called The Pamela Anderson effect. Now, I'm not saying all men, but 999.9% do fit in this category. They want a woman who looks good, has a great body and can take care of them in their old age. I, of course do NOT fit any of the above. I have no boobs, my body is so so, and I can't cook physically (now I can tell you how to cook verbally). Let's face it, I'm lacking in the beauty department. And I know my family and friends are going to say no to this fact, they are going to say you are beautiful the way you are, but they're my family and friends. They don't want to hurt me.

I have had many infatuations and affairs with men throughout my life, but I can honestly say I have been in love only twice.

To begin this, I need to say, I have always dreamt of these men right before I met them. This is a true fact. The first love was A, and yes, I am changing their name to protect their innocence. I met A when I was 16. He worked at my school. I can still remember the first time I saw him. I was rolling into the MPR (multipurpose room) and he was with my friend. He was nice, funny and could do everything. I think the first thing I said to him was "Are you married?" He said. "Yes." and I said, "Damn!!!" We both laughed. We instantly bonded. We had so much fun together and we could always talk about anything. A saw me through my adolescence and that was not easy for me. We always had that special connection. I couldn't believe how sweet his heart could be and how he treated every one of us with compassion and respect.

A was married three times. I couldn't believe his bad luck with women. Each one had mental issues and not very nice. After I graduated from high school, we still continued to be friends. He would come to my apartment and we would watch TV, go out to a movie or go to the park. He would fix things in my apartment to make it easier for me. He made an inhaler holder that was fixed to my headboard so I could use my inhaler independently in case I had an asthma attack in the middle of the night.

A was a musician and played the guitar. He would play at school and for me. (Keep the musician part in mind. It's going to be a recurring theme throughout my life, even to this day.)

A and I formed decades of friendship, love and sex, but that will come later.

Dear She
You don't know who I am.
I don't know who you are.
But, I need to tell you She, how lucky you are.
You have a gift from God; a treasure not easily found.
He is a friendship in my life, someone that I adore.
But, how I wish it was more.
How I wish that I was that, I was the She He loves.
How I wish that I was the She that He goes home to.
When He speaks of She.
How I wish the She was Me.
But, don't worry She, for you are the She that He loves.
I am not an intimidation.
Nor, do I want to be.
He is only in my dreams at night.
But, He is in your life every day.

How lucky you are She. Be proud of who you are She. Because you are the She that He loves.

After high school, I went to college. The Department of Vocational Rehabilitation was paying for my schooling. I had to take one semester off due to some financial issues.

You know, it's funny how God plans things so perfectly on his time. At that time in my life, I was still under the school system. I was still seeing the school's orthopedic doctors for my developmental needs. So, one day Mom and I went back to school for my annual checkup. Since I had just graduated one year before, most of the staff knew me and when they found out that I was just sitting at home, this was not OK with them at all. They asked me to come back and help out. The secretary took just five minutes to set up the bus to start picking me up the following Monday. This was going to be like an internship for me until I went back to college in the following semester. Little did I know, I would meet the love of my life.

I was glad to go back. I was bored at my house, I needed something to do and besides, A was there too. That night, I had a dream again. I dreamt of a man.

The very first day, I went to the room where the assistants hung out. My friend Lee was there. Lee was in charge of matching up the aides to the kids each day. In turn, the aides would be assigned to help the kids in feeding and other needs they might have. Lee said "So, you're back, huh?" I said "Yeah, for a while, till next semester starts." At that moment, he came in. He was tall, dark and oh so handsome with lots of muscles. Lee said, "Santa meet R, and R meet Santa, be careful with her, she's wild!" I said "Leeeee!", with a bashful face. Lee then said, "I think I'm going to put you two together. R, will you help Santa with her lunch?" R said yes. So, in the MPR, as he was feeding me my PB&J sandwich, I decided that I was done with the sandwich and wanted to move on to my dessert. I indicated to R that I wanted that sweet roll right in front of me. R said "No, you need to eat all of your food, before you can eat your dessert." My old friend was sitting right beside me, and I said to him "Who is this asshole, telling me what to do?" After all, I was nineteen and I thought I was hot shit. During the next few weeks, R and I started talking and getting to know each other. R was a body builder and in a band, (a musician and drummer). R was going to expose me to new things I had never known before. What a great guy! R was nice, funny and I liked how he made me feel. There was something developing, but I really didn't know what.

It was December 1981, and Christmas break was coming up. Also, I knew that I was heading back to college in January. I knew that I wasn't going to see R or, for that matter, A anymore. There are some people that you can't say good bye to and not have a little piece of your heart just break. I knew this about R. On one of the last days, I gave R my address and number and said "If you're not busy, maybe you can stop by some time," really not knowing if he was taking me seriously or not.

> *"There are people that walk across your heart lightly, Then they are people that leave foot prints."*

Usually, for a Hispanic family like mine, Christmas time is Tamale-making time. This process takes a few days to prepare, so my Mom and I were waiting for my sister Rosie to come by to start our yearly ritual. I went to my bedroom to get something when I heard a knock at the door. "Oh, It's Rosie," I thought. Mom came in and said, "Santa, there's a guy at the door, looking for you!" Who? Not a lot of guys came around looking for me. It was R. R said "I had a bad day and wanted to see you." A surprised look was on my face. He met my mom and when my dad came home with groceries, he helped my dad with them.

My mom had asked R to stay for dinner, but R said,"No, I need to go." Before he left, he said, "Can we go out some time?" I said yeah! Within the next few days, we had talked on the phone and made plans to go on a date.

At this point in my life, I had never been on a "real" date before. Sure I had boyfriends in high school, but never went on dates. I was so excited and scared. Mom and I picked out a cute little conservative outfit. R had called and asked if we could stop by his house to meet his mom and sister. My first date with a very handsome man and I was going to meet his family too!!!!! I was so nervous.

As we were heading to his house, I kept wondering what his mother would say. Now, I wasn't the type of girl a guy's mom would welcome with open arms. That disapproval sentiment by anyone outside my family was weighing on my heart. Would she accept and/or like me I thought? But R's mom was so different. She was so nice and inviting and his sister was awesome too.

This was a big test. Could I just become a woman on her first date, and not worry that my disabilities would get in the way? R's mom and sister had made me feel that my disability had disappeared. They could understand me and my wheelchair was not an issue. I couldn't believe it. R wanted to show me where he practiced playing his drums. I excused us and she smiled.

We went to see a movie called "Whose Life is it Anyway" with Richard Dreyfess. R put me in a seat next to him.
As we watched the movie, he held my hand!!!! Wow. After the movie, we went walking/rolling on the pier. I felt so comfortable and free!

I was getting cold and we got back in the car. We talked and I asked him, "Do you have a girlfriend?" He said, "Yes." I can still remember hitting the side of the car door thinking to myself, "Damn! He's only going to be my friend." But then R said, "I'm not happy with her, I can't talk to her the way that I can talk to you." And at that moment……..we kissed!!!!! Wow!!!! I went home that night with the biggest smile on my face. A few days later, I found out that he had broken up with his girlfriend.

During the next few days, I met all of his friends and the guys in the band. I was a little intimidated, not knowing how much R had told them about me or my disability, but much to my surprise, they were very nonchalant about the whole chick in the wheelchair thing. All of them treated me as one of them. I will always appreciate that.

As I mentioned before, R was a body builder and the gym was very important to him, as it is to any body builder. The first time he took me there, I felt so out of place, so out of my element. Suddenly, I saw my disability as a barrier to this relationship. This was a barrier more than everything else: a new family, meeting his friends, my parents being unsure about the whole boyfriend thing and my insecurities about me. This was the thing that could end this.

That night, as R was taking me home, I started to cry. I told R that this was never going to work. I told him you need a better woman, someone who you can do stuff with. R just held me and told me it's going to be Ok. R never saw my disability; he only saw me.

When we met, I was still a virgin. I had that Old Catholic mind-set that my Mom had instilled in me from a young age that sex before marriage was a sin and I would have a "reputation" of being a bad girl if I had sex before marriage. Blah Blah blah. R said he would wait for me until I was ready. Poor R, I made him wait six months. Now, that doesn't mean that we did not do stuff, because we did!!!! R was my teacher in sex. He taught me the difference between making love and having sex. We experimented and tried things that I had never done. We talked about birth control and what the best method would be for us. One time, when we were being intimate, R stopped, pulled out a condom, and said, "This is a condom." As he opened the package, he let me ask questions.

What kind of man would do that for his woman? Not many that I know. But R was like that. He was the sweetest man. He would do things just to make me happy. It was the early 80's and MTV was brand new. There was a concert I wanted to watch, but I wasn't going to see R that night. But that night, R shows up at my door saying, "I know you wanted to see that concert, let's go see it and I'll bring you back." Other times, he would just pop up at school, just to say "Hi." That was the kind of the man he was and that's why I fell in love with him.

R and I stayed together for three years, and then it was over. R never really did tell me why we broke up, but I think it was because of my disability. Maybe he just got tired of taking care of me, or maybe he wanted more that I could ever offer. Either way, R gave me the best three years of my life. No one will ever compare in my heart, except for a little boy named Noah. That story would come much later.

I finished college and was living in my own apartment. A had known about my break up with R and started to come over again. For the first time, we both were single and started a sexual relationship, something we both knew would happen if we ever got the chance, and at that time, we had that chance. We both knew that our relationship wasn't going to be permanent. We could just be together and then he would go home. That was Ok with me. I loved A, but too much A wasn't good for me. I think we both felt that way about each other.

I met Tim while I was working at my first job at UCP. I was the administrative assistant at the time. Tim applied to be the computer teacher at the day program. He was very educated and had his career working with people with developmental disabilities and intellectual disabilities. He was nice.

Tim had a different way of thinking and I was intrigued, but he had a very unique way about him. When he didn't want to do something, he wouldn't do it and this made me mad.

There are so many bad things I can say about Tim, but I don't want to. I would rather focus on the better side of Tim.

I need to tell you that this relationship with Tim has been the longest and the hardest relationship I have had with a man.

We have been friends for 26 years. When we first started dating it was nice, but I noticed that he was not as experienced in the relationship department. He had told me he had only been with one woman before me. Sex was very awkward and frustrating. Tim had told me that he was gay from the very start, but I thought that he was just inexperienced and somehow, I could "help" him. I was so naive. We got engaged and I thought that it would fix everything. But something was not right.

Usually, the bride-to-be will be happy in planning her wedding. I imagined picking out bridesmaid dresses with my sister Stella, (my maid of honor). I could see my brother, Tony strolling me down the aisle. I dreamt of my wedding dress. That white lacey gown that fitted to my body, and had accents in the front, so that it wouldn't hurt my back. It would have the right padding that complemented my small bosoms, and a veil that wasn't so long that it would get caught in my wheels, but long enough to be pretty. Purple flowers would be everywhere.

But something was not right. I couldn't get into the wedding thing. I wouldn't say that Tim and I were unhappy, but we weren't happy either. I called off the wedding. We still lived together (even to this day), but we are not a couple.

We have many, many ups and downs in our relationship, but somehow we work it out. Tim puts up with my shit and I put up with his shit. The best thing about Tim is, he is my greatest advocate. He pushes me to do things that I don't think I can do. Tim is the catalyst in my career as an advocate. Tim gives me the freedom to do what I want, but that can be good or bad sometimes.

We both have had affairs with men, but no man has ever come between us.

The common thing that we both wanted was to be parents. When we were a couple, we tried for four years to get pregnant, but it never worked. We even went to see a specialist. She said his boys swam backwards and I had an enzyme that was too low. The doctor had suggested fertility therapy, but I never liked getting shots. Anyway, I figured it would be up to God at that point.

In 1996, we moved to Las Vegas and got off to a rocky start for the first two years. We finally had gotten good jobs and I was able to buy a house. My house, this was something I had always wanted, my biggest achievement so far. It wasn't a big house, but it was my house.

Now, you must be thinking, she's was talking about men, why is she now talking about her house? Wait you guys, there's a reason!

Anyway, Tim and I were working at a shelter workshop. I was running the computer lab for the clients and Tim was a service coordinator that worked mainly with the staff. Tim had befriended a man named Ken. Soon thereafter, Ken was coming to our apartment and when we finally got the keys to my house, Ken was the first person to start packing us for the big move. We would pick him up each weekend and he would stay with us. Ken would make the weekends fun again, something that Tim couldn't do. One day, Tim went out and Ken and I were alone. We were packing and laughing, and then we just started to kiss and make out. Soon after that it turned into a full affair. Tim knew about this and he was kind of happy for me. Tim knew that Ken could provide me with something that he couldn't and that was a man's touch.

Ken was kind of a shyster, always making deals with people, but I didn't really care. He was providing me with what I needed.........sex. I knew that the relationship wasn't going to last long. After about two years, I got bored. I had decided to call it off. Then, something happened that I wasn't expecting, I was expecting!!!!!!!

Many years later, Tim had told me that he had asked Ken to get me pregnant. Ok, it wasn't the ideal situation, but Tim and I really wanted a baby so bad! Ken was the only option. Ken stayed around for two more years, and then he was gone. I have nothing but gratitude towards Ken. Ken gave me my heart back. Ken gave me Noah.

One Hundred and One Ways to Heat A Burrito

IN 1985, I MOVED INTO my own apartment. I began going to Cal State University, Northridge, and decided not to live in the dorms at school due to having to move in and out every semester. I had applied for section 8 housing, was approved and found an apartment near school. It was close enough that if I wanted, I could roll to school or, on rainy days, I could take one bus.

This was a huge deal for me and my Mom. I had been living at home all my life and my Mom and I had become even more inseparable since my Dad's death. I knew that I needed to try to live on my own and besides; I felt that it was time for my Mom to live her own life too.

I guess I had planned to move out years before I did, because I had started to collect things for the apartment: pots and pans, towels, bed sheets, etc.

My apartment was great. I felt so grownup and free. The first few days were a little scary. At night, every sound I heard, I would get out of bed and find where that sound was coming from then go back to bed. I think I got up around ten times those nights.

My new PCA (Personal Care Assistant) Celia was coming for the first time in the morning. I was a little angry because Mom had hired her without me even meeting her. It's a funny thing for me, when you hire someone that you know is going to know every intimate detail about you. It can be daunting. People are different and the PCA and myself had to learn each other's ways of doing things, like direct care. There are some people who are patient and some who are not. Modesty goes out the window when you have a disability. If I had a dime for everyone that has seen my ass, I would be rich!

Lucky for my Mom, Celia and I got along great and we soon got into a daily routine. Celia was a small lady, but mighty. I swear she could have me showered, dressed, fed and ready to go in one hour. Celia only came in the morning and in the evening, which meant I had to fend for myself during the day.

At school it was easy. There were people who would help me if I needed to go to the bathroom or got hungry, but at home, I had to find ways to take care of myself. One of biggest hurdles for me was drinking from a straw. Growing up, everyone would just raise a cup to my mouth with a towel under my chin, but now there was no one to raise that cup. The straw method was hard to learn and very messy, but if I wanted to drink, I had to force myself to learn.

I don't think many people know the variations of straws available. There are textures, lengths, and flexibility. Not all straws are made equal. I needed to find one that would be strong enough that when I clenched down on it, it wouldn't collapse. I even wrote a 5-page report for school about the variations of straws.

The other big obstacle was eating lunch. Since I couldn't use my hands to prepare food and then eat it, in the typical way, I needed to find my own way to eat. My BFF, Susy, had her own apartment too. I would go to her home and watch her do things without using her hands. She could open a soda can, heat food in a microwave and eat by herself. I watched her technique, how she could hold a plate in her teeth and gently put it into the microwave. I knew I could do this too, but in my own way.

> Santa's way to eat a Burrito
> Using my hands, I would take out burrito from freezer and place it on counter.
> I would manipulate the wrapper by biting the paper off and would put it into a plastic bag with handles.
> I would put the bag in the microwave with the

handles facing out making sure that the handles were in front by the door.

When the burrito was cooked, I would take out the bag with the handle away from the body by extending my arm as far away as I could and would take it to the table.

I would spread the towel on the table.

I would take out the burrito and put it on the towel by turning the bag over using my mouth.

I could then eat the burrito, taking bites at each end, no hands required.

Not a pretty sight, but hey, I could eat.

Susy and I would go out for lunch and eat the only way we could. Some people didn't like the way we ate, but I figure, they can always offer to help us.

If you have a disability, you need to learn tricks to make your life easier. For example, for women, have extra underwear with pads already in them, so you just change the underwear, and would not worry about putting the pad on correctly. I had swim shoes in the shower to lessen the risks of slipping. I always had opened canned drinks in the refrigerator door, so drinks can stay cold and you can take a sip without moving the can. A little unconventional, yes, but it works!

I lived in my apartment for 11 years. Sometimes it was lonely, but I had my fun too!

The Story of Noah

In 2001, my world changed. Here is an account of what happened.

Well, here I am, I think to myself as everyone is buzzing around me. Dr. Litt is checking me down below and making sure that he has all the right paraphernalia to do the job. Mom is becoming animated preparing for what's to come. Stella and Tim are both hoisting up a leg and Tony is giving a play-by-play account with his video camera.

"This is it" I thought, the moment where everything changes, where my life as one, becomes two. When my selfishness stops and his love begins.

This is a miracle from God, the one that I've wished for all of my life and have dreamed about constantly. The dream that I put away in my secret place and only thought of when I fantasized or found out that someone else was going to have a little one.

Nine months ago, my main focus was, "I'm going to Washington." I wanted to become the advocate for the state of Nevada. I was thinking of people who I could ask to write letters of recommendation and talking to my boss about taking time off, making plans.

Isn't it funny how one little trip to the drug store can change your whole perspective on everything! A little white stick was about to navigate the rest of my life and that stick was positive. Disbelief sat in.

"How?" I asked. All my doctors told me that this might never happen, and for thirty-eight years, they were right.

I didn't know if I should be happy or sad. Should I be looking forward to this or finding a way out? I thought about Tim, how much this would impact him. He already looks so tired with just taking care of me and now someone else would be even more dependent on him than me. The good thing was that Tim always wanted to be a dad, just as much as I wanted to be a mom. Two wishes for the price for one.

When I told my family, they were less than thrilled. Some even suggested an abortion, which was the easy way out. Mom got sick with worry. I could see their concerns. This was unknown territory, even for me. I had a very active life up until now, especially for a woman with a significant disability. There was nothing I did not try, at least once. But this was something surprising, scary, unimaginable, and new.

I always knew there were women with disabilities who had children, but I'd never known any. I never knew how they dealt with the day-to-day parenting skills they needed to have. Do I have those skills, and if I don't, how do I get them?

For the first time, I was worried that my "disability" would become my "handicap" in being a mom. And so the search began for any information I could find. There is not a lot out there for new parents with disabilities. I found the organization *Through the Looking Glass*. They had a lot of good information but they were in Berkeley, California. I bought every book they had, and talked to a wonderful woman named Judy, who also has CP and is a mom.

So, I called all my friends, many of whom were also my colleagues, and asked them for help. They were not just going to watch me eat like a pig and rub my tummy. Together we would form a team, a circle of brains that can think and problem solve. There were things to plan for and adaptive equipment to create, looking for unique solutions to unique problems. The things that I needed were not at "Babies R Us," although I love that store and they have some great stuff, which can be adapted. Every month, we would meet and make a plan of action. Each team member would take a piece of the puzzle and try to make it fit before the next meeting. Poor baby, not even born yet and already he had meetings to attend.

Even though, we could not solve all my concerns, it gave me peace of mind to know that I had the ongoing support when I called for HELP! This is an evolving process, which will continue until Noah is 99 or so.

I picked the name Noah because it means comfort, silence, devout love, and most of all strong to be in my body. He needed to be strong to be in my body. He learned from the beginning that Mommy's body moves in many different ways and he had to go with the flow, (no pun intended).

I had a normal pregnancy, which was a shock even to me. Although I was considered a high-risk patient, Dr. Litt was very nonchalant about the whole "pregnant woman in a wheelchair" thing. I thought that I would have to see my doctor so often that we would become bosom buddies, but that was not the case. Even my own low expectations were blown away. It was a pregnancy as usual with the everyday cravings, then barfing, the constant kicking of my ribs, and the everlasting heartburn.

For the whole nine months, everything was going smooth. My CP didn't really play a significant part, except for as I/(Noah) got bigger, my hips couldn't quite figure out how to hold me up while I was standing. I remember swishing from hip to hip trying to balance myself.

It was almost my due date and at my last Doctor's appointment, Dr. Litt said, "Hey, I'm going to be the attending doctor at the hospital next Tuesday, since I'm going be there, why don't you be there and we can all be there and we can have a baby together. I will induce labor." Dr. Litt called the hospital himself and made all the arrangements.

That Monday night, we had everything packed and ready to go. As Tim was getting me ready for bed, he stated "Santa, you're already in labor". "No I'm not", I informed Tim, and thought, what a crazy man. I couldn't sleep and I was praying for five o'clock to come.

The morning came and I was anxious to go the hospital. As we were leaving, I looked around my house, thinking that the next time I come in this house our home will be completely different. Another new human being would call this place home and we would have new names, Mommy and Daddy.

At the hospital, they were already waiting for me. Nurse Janet was assigned to me. She would be my right hand man for the rest of the day. As she was checking me, she claimed, "You are four centimeters dilated. Santa, you can get an epidural now." I said, "No, not yet." Oh, naive me. My sister Stella was going to be my labor coach and when she got there, nothing was really happening. The monitors kept on indicating that I was having contractions, but I didn't feel them. Nurse Janet would come in and remind me that I could have my epidural any time, but I really felt fine. So, in my naïve, inexperienced little brain, I'm thinking "Hey, maybe I can do this without any meds." Yeah right!

It was around 12:00 noon and still nothing. Stella and Tim said, "Let's blow this joint and go have lunch." Mom had stayed with me. At 1:00 p.m. it happened! I had the biggest bad ass contraction. Noah was getting ready to make his debut appearance. My mom kept saying, "Breathe, Santa, breathe."

Now, remember I said that my CP hadn't played any part in my pregnancy? Well now it did. It's a well known fact that if a person with CP gets startled, cold, hurt, or nervous, their body becomes rigid. It's like its saying to the body, "What the Hell????" With that first contraction, my body was telling me, what the hell and get it out. Nurse Janet strolls in and says, "I can see things have changed, would you like that epidural now?" I said, "Yes please," nodding my head up and down profusely. Now nurse Janet says, "Well, you're going to have to wait a little; the anesthesiologist just went for an emergency C-section. He'll be by after he is done." After what felt like an eternity, the anesthesiologist (God) came in. He said "I see you're in pain, let me help you." He also said, "Now you need to hold perfectly still so I can put the needle in your spine." Now, having CP and being able to hold perfectly still is an oxymoron.

I'm not a sports fan, but I learned what a football huddle was, because everyone piled on top of me. Tim lay on top of me, curving my body, while everyone else grabbed a limb and held it down. I was praying, God, just let the needle go in. I'll do anything, you want, just let the needle go in. Then finally ahhhh, instant relief. I was so happy!!!!

Dr. Litt came in and said, "Let's have a baby! It's time for you to push". I noticed that the epidural was working, maybe working too well, because I wasn't feeling anything. I was just going through the motions of grunting and pushing. Finally, Dr. Litt says "I can see you need a little help". He pulls out what looked like a tiny Yamaka with a big syringe. He said, "I'm going to pull on the next contraction."

So, here I am, just minutes from becoming someone's "Mom." I'm thinking to myself, I sure hope he likes me. All the preparing, speculating, anticipating, throwing up, Braxton Hicks contractions, baby showers, getting the nursery set up, being too tired to do anything, next doctor's appointment, packing bags for the hospital (don't forget the camera), praying, and worrying are now coming to an end.

And one more push…HAPPY BIRTHDAY: NOAH!

And so the story of Noah begins…

Raising Noah

Before I had my son, Noah, I wondered what kind of a Mom I would be. I knew that I wanted to be as involved as I possibly could in his care. I also knew that I could not do everything I wanted to do without help, at least for the first few years.

Although 90% of the physical child care was done by Tim and others, I needed to inform all other caretakers that "I" was MOM and I made all the decisions where Noah was concerned.

I needed to find ways for Noah and me to form that mother and child bond. The first project to conquer was breast feeding. Everyone kept telling me that the bottle would be better for feeding Noah since everyone else was assisting, but this was the only thing that I could have with Noah that was truly ours. I found breast feeding easier on my waterbed. The way that the mattress would rise on one side, just the right height for Noah's head to be parallel to my breast. I must admit he was a great sucker and when he could find that nipple, he would clench on for dear life. When I was in my wheelchair, I used lots of pillows all around me. For me, sitting like an Indian against the armrest of my couch was neat and a safe way to breast feed Noah. Nursing pillows (especially the ones with the back support) are great and useful for support in positioning mommy and baby. I breast fed Noah for six weeks and then I was done. It got to be very tiring and my breasts hurt a lot! But I still wanted Noah to get the great nutrients that my milk could give him. The breast pump was a God send. I could give my baby my/his milk, but no pain was involved. We did the breast pump thing for about three more months, and then we moved on to baby formula.

Since my CP hands would not allow me to hold a baby bottle in the typical way, we had to improvise. Again, I was determined to play the mommy role as much as I could. Baby bouncers were the key to keeping Noah upright and safe, but there was the holding the bottle thing. We tried many different types of bottles, but they never seemed to work out quite right. Finally, the puppet master came. My good friend and mentor Dr. Colleen Thoma had brought Noah a gift. It was a big round fluffy pink pig. It was cute and cuddly. Little did anyone know that big round fluffy pig was going to become assistive technology. I had trouble holding bottles. The diameter was too big for my hands to grasp, but the place where you normally put your hand in the puppet, was perfect for a baby bottle. I found that I could hold that pig's hand or foot and keep the bottle in place for Noah.

When Noah got a little older, it was baby food time and of course, I didn't want to miss out on that either. So, the problem was going to be. How was I going to hold a baby spoon, when I couldn't hold a spoon to feed myself? There are many things that I could do with my head and mouth that I couldn't do with my hands. I had a friend who was a physical therapist. Together we created foam spoons. I could hold the spoon in my mouth. I must admit it was a little tricky at first, but after a while, I got the hang of it. The right high chair was the key. We discovered that the height of the chair was very important. Most high chairs have a little foot rest in the middle. I found it to be a hinder because I couldn't get close enough to Noah's mouth, so we just took it off. If I was higher than Noah, then we had more success in getting the food in his mouth and not on him, or me, or the floor, or the ceiling, or the dog. I knew that Noah much preferred Daddy feeding, less mess, but I still needed to have that human touch.

I discovered that the floor was an even playground and almost everything we did was on the floor. We could get him dressed, exercise him, play peek-a-boo and discover toys together and I felt safe.

When Noah was an infant, I used a baby sling to carry him around. I felt like an Indian woman with her little papoose. As he grew, he learned how to hold on to mommy's wheelchair as we rode. To this day, Noah is a wiz in wheelchair-ology. He knows what every part is and what it does. I know now what a taxi driver feels like, because when he hops on the footplates, we go! It has gotten to the point where I don't drive anymore, he does. I'm just the passenger. One of our favorite things that was only ours was going to the market. The market was on the corner and we could get there in minutes. Tim would put a big bag in the back and Noah on my lap and we would go. The neighborhood knew us by name. At the market, we would do our own thing. I would tell Noah what to get from the shelves and he would get them. Sometimes the items were too high and Noah played acrobat and climbed on the armrest on my chair to get the items. It was fun and, of course, Noah got special treats. At the checkout counter, Noah would place the item on the counter and get the money out of my side pouch. Together the clerk and Noah would put everything in the big bag and Noah, with some kind of candy in hand, and we would contently ride home.

Bath time was always a fun time. We soon discovered if I got in the tub along with him I could do more. Keeping Noah safe was a challenge. We first tried the round bath seat, but it slipped away and was not steady enough. So, I found out that if I wrapped my legs around Noah, he was not going anywhere. I think Noah liked my strong legs around him. He knew that he can still play and still feel safe. I am proud to say that I (not dad) taught my son how to wash his hair, clean his body, brush his teeth and scrub those knees.

As I said earlier, I could not do a lot of personal care for Noah when he was an infant. Tim (Dad) and others did most of the physical care giving. When Tim had to go back to work and (eventually me too), we had to hire a baby sitter. It was hard for me to watch and have another woman do the child care. For every person we interviewed, I would tell them "My Rules." I needed them to understand that "I" was MOM and no one else was going to be.

I learned that being a good parent didn't mean I needed to be a physical parent. Being a good parent means being there, even if it's only for changing a diaper. I could talk to him and play with him. I could verbally teach vs. physical teach. One example was punching a straw into a juice box. Noah couldn't quite get the sticking the straw into that pouch. So, we would use the tip of pen to open the hole. I would tell him, "push the pen," then the hole would start and he could put the straw in.

When Noah was around three, Noah's care giver got sick. We knew that we needed to find alternate care and really, it was time for Noah to be socialized with other kids. Tim and I decided to put Noah into day care. We were lucky. We found a day care center three blocks away from our home, which meant that I could take Noah back and forth in my wheelchair. I was a little worried about how the staff and teachers were going to react to the mom in wheelchair thing, but they were very accommodating and welcoming. At first, the teachers and kids didn't know what to think. His teachers were great! The first day as we rolled in, she announced to her class, Ok, Noah's mom is in a wheelchair, who has questions? I let them look at my chair but, after days, weeks, and months, the newness slowly went away and the kids didn't stop and stare, and I was only known as just Noah's Mom. I don't think Noah had a clue why the other kids stared, and sometimes were afraid of me. After all, Mom and the wheelchair were typical for him.

The question: I knew that BIG question was going to come. So, in my mind, I had rehearsed and rehearsed how I was going to tell Noah where babies come from. So, one day, while watching Scooby Doo, Noah says, Mom, I have a question? Ok, I thought, I'm ready!!!! Well, the other mommies walk, and you don't? Why he said. I felt that baseball bat hit me. Wow, I thought that question would come much later in his life. Well, I said, when mommy was born, I got a booboo in my head and I couldn't walk. Oh, he said, and continued to watch Scooby Doo. Naturally, as the years went by, that explanation got more detailed.

Disciplining Noah is all my duty. Tim tries, but really, I have that power. No need to be physical, when this "Moms Look" can get him going. Noah understands every word I say the first time, especially when I'm angry. I learned that if I'm angry, and don't talk to him for a while, that's worse than any other punishment I can give him.

Now that Noah is a teenager, more challenges are on the way. But I must admit I've been lucky, Noah is not a bad kid, with little bumps along the way, but nothing major. I don't really tell him what to do. I explain to him what I don't like and tell him why. He usually heeds my advice.

I love how Noah picks his friends. He has an eclectic group. I would like to think that since many different people come and go through my door, Noah has a good sense of people who are good, who are not so good. His friends always treat me with respect. They may not understand me, but they know what I say (with Noah's interpreting, of course). Noah lives in a very inclusive world.

And the girls are coming.

Becoming An Advocate

I THINK I'VE ALWAYS BEEN an advocate, even when the word "advocate" did not exist.

I have always said how I felt, asked for what I wanted and always asked "Why." Maybe it was the people in my life that saw me as a leader and encouraged me, or maybe it was just me being curious and wanting to live my life the way I choose. My Dad's death had a real impact on me. I realized that my parents were not going to live forever and I didn't want to live with my siblings and become "their child." Even though I knew they would welcome me with open arms, I knew I had my own path to follow.

Life can be difficult for a person with a significant disability and from what I had experienced throughout my life, I knew I wanted to make a difference for people with disabilities' lives in teaching self-advocacy. In the early 90's, I met two women, Barbara and Sherry, who worked at Children's Hospital in Los Angeles. They were working on a project on Self Advocacy. Their task was to get a group of people with developmental disabilities and intellectual disabilities to create a product that would promote and teach Self-Advocacy. This group would be charged with every aspect in producing this product. We chose to make a video called "Robert's Choice" and it had a companion training curriculum. We made the decisions on everything, from writing the script to hiring the actors and directing the production. I was in charge of editing the training curriculum's handbook. We did everything; Barbara and Sherry were only there for support and to give advice. This was my first experience in speaking with my voice and feeling that I had value in what I thought. I also learned the power of being in a group of advocates and creating a tool that would teach others about Self-Advocacy. They also introduced me to the People First movement and invited me to a meeting. I quickly got involved in the movement and started to build People First chapters in LA.

I liked this organization and the work. I saw that people with developmental disabilities and intellectual disabilities (DD/IDD) were finally having a voice in their own lives and were starting to take charge.

But, I think I didn't really start my advocacy career until I moved to Las Vegas in the mid 90's. I found out there were no People First chapters or, for that matter, no advocacy groups in Nevada. This was not acceptable to me and I needed to do something about it. I had met the Director of our Desert Regional Center (DRC) and he was pretty open to the idea of starting up a support group for people with developmental disabilities and intellectual disabilities. Some of the community providers and DRC staff were all in and supported us.

People First of Nevada started. I was so excited to teach Self-Advocacy skills to other people. It was great, but the membership started to dwindle down. We had invited every provider to bring their people to the monthly meetings. I soon realized that if the staff were not interested in coming, they would not encourage their people to go. People First lasted about a year, then it died. I was heartbroken, but knew that somehow it would come back.

One of the providers, Lila, had become my friend and she was the first person who started introducing me to the disability community in Nevada. She told me about an ad in the paper calling for people with disabilities and parents to apply for class called Partners in Policy Making. I applied, and got a letter from the Director which stated that I didn't get in that year, but please apply again next year. So I did and got in the next class.

Partners in Policy Making is an eight-month class that meets one weekend per month. Depending on the program, the participants stay overnight to do intense networking with the other participants. The course is for people with disabilities and parents or siblings of kids with disabilities. Each class covers a different topic: from early intervention, the history of disability, to the school system, to assistive technology, to social services to guardianship, we covered it all. It's like disability 101 on steroids. The homework was intense too, but the people that I met made it so invaluable. The members of this group would become my lifelong friends and my allies in the disability world.

I don't know why, but I went to class without any communication device or anyone to interpret for me. I winged it. Some of the parents were new to the field and didn't know what to think about me. They were intimidated to talk to me, which is funny to me because I'm only 4`10" and couldn't hurt a fly.

One person in particular was Mary Bryant. On the first day, we needed to introduce ourselves to another person. As Mary says it: She was so nervous to talk to me. She was worried that she wouldn't be able to understand me. When we got to sit together, I noticed she was sweating. But despite our rough start, this was the beginning of a powerful and long-lasting friendship.

At the same time, Mary started work at the University of Nevada, Reno, at the Nevada Center for Excellence in Disabilities. She started a new program. Mary was a great grant writer. She wrote a grant to the Corporation for National and Community Service, Americorps*VISTA

(Volunteers in Service to America). The members were hired to coordinate a new Self-Advocacy/Self-Determination Project, via People First of Nevada. What was unique about this project was all of VISTA members had disabilities. The VISTAS lived in different locations of Nevada. This was important as they could work in their own community and start a People First chapter. When it came down to hiring a VISTA for Las Vegas, Mary hired me, without an interview. Within the first three years we established our 501c3, got three chapters up and running and started making our voices heard in the legislation realm. People First would initiate three bills, the Signature Stamp bill, the People First Respectful Language bill, and the Rosa Law (which we assisted in passing).

Everything was clicking into place and I felt fulfilled. People First was exploding in Nevada. I was with VISTA for five years and became the Statewide President. The UCED hired me to be part of their staff as an advisor. Many people were proud of me, but most importantly, I was proud of myself. I felt valued and I had purpose.

The UCED had also introduced me to The Nevada Governor's Council on Developmental Disabilities. Mary had become the Chair and asked me to start attending meetings. Soon after, I applied to become a member. I waited a year, then I was appointed by the Governor. Both the UCED and The Nevada Governor's Council on

Developmental Disabilities had exposed me to the National level of the disability issues, which I can proudly say I am a part of to this day.

After working for the UCED for seven years, The Nevada Governor's Council on Developmental Disabilities contracted with me to work on different grants throughout the years. Again, someone had seen my value and not my disability. The problem was and still is to this day, finding a job in the community. Even if I have an impressive resume, most employers won't even look at me. They see the wheelchair and unflattering appearance and they assume that the woman and the resume is not the same person in life. I have been to the Department of Rehabilitation (VR) four times and to this day, they have never helped me get a job. I always felt that the clients have to become circus animals, always needing to jump through hoops and always seeking that fine line of acceptance. There is always that person who has that "look," you just know what they are saying silently, "This person will never get a job." Even when there are new laws (that I helped write), there is that invisible line which people with developmental disabilities and intellectual disabilities can't cross.

This is why people with developmental disabilities and intellectual disabilities need to be more involved in society, in everything: community, education, and the political atmosphere; we need to come to the table, not as voiceless tokens, but rather as active, opinionated and confident participants.

I sit on many committees, both State and Federal. I love being involved in the movement. I love contributing in making changes to the disability system that make lives better for generations to come. The only regret is, many times, I am the only one with a disability at the table. There should be more advocates with different cultures, experiences and options as well. My life has not been that typical as my other friends. They need to be at the table as well. Let's face it, this gal is getting old and it's time for young blood to come in.

At the Federal level, it is getting better. They are finally seeing us as a part of the American fabric. We have talents and gifts to share and want to have our American dream.

I am an advocate because I have a big mouth and I want to teach people that they don't have to live by the status quo, that if they have big dreams, they should go for them. No one is better than you and you are not less than them.

An "X" Does Not Mark the Spot

BEING A PERSON WITH SUFFICIENT disabilities does have its disadvantages. The pure simple task of signing your own name can become an ordeal when signing business and legal documents, such as, getting an ID at the DMV, opening a bank account, buying your first home or voting. I find it degrading when "they" say "oh, just make an "X" or a mark (like chicken scratch) and that will be ok." But the mark is not my signature. I am not a chicken and that mark won't be the same the next time I make it.

A signature stamp is a stamp that I had made at an office supply store. I needed to write my name three times and from those three signatures, they made the stamp off of the best signature I provided. Ok, somebody had to help me to create a signature, but after that creative signature was created, it was all mine and everyone knew it by sight. I even had my bank write up an affidavit identifying that this stamp was my valid and legal signature. I started using my signature stamp when I turned 18 years old and had never had a problem with it until I moved to Nevada. The first time I felt the punch was when I tried to get my ID from the NV DMV. They wanted me to sign my name into this little box. Yeah Right! Like I could write anything into a little box. I kept telling them that I had a signature stamp and that was my valid and legal signature, but the NV DMV wouldn't hear of it. I reluctantly made a mark with help.

The second nightmarish event was when I was buying my house. After weeks of looking at house after house, negotiating prices and a tree of paperwork, the biggest obstacle I had was the signature stamp. Finally, the mortgage company had everyone in the world sign a paper stating that the signature stamp was legitimate.

The last straw was when I went to vote, another simple undertaking I thought as a good citizen. This became a huge challenge. The polling place could not accept my signature stamp as a "natural signature," and they wanted me to sign my name into that little box. They said that I could use the whole page if I had to, so, I did. I had always thought somebody should make a law about using alternative methods when writing one's name, but never pursued it.

One night, while sitting with Tom Allman, a representative from Nevada Disability And Law Center, waiting for a People First meeting to begin, I told Tom about my plead. I told him that something should be done about using a stamp for a legal signature, but I didn't really know how to proceed. He listened intently and wrote something on a little piece of paper and said "I will see about this." Ok, I thought, he will probably forget or misplace that paper, or something else, but at least he was nice about it.

A few weeks later, I get this e-mail from Tom, stating that he had talked to Jack Mayes, the director of NDALC and they wanted to pursue this subject. They had done some research and found that the state of Minnesota and other states had laws regarding signature stamps for people with disabilities. Wow, I thought! This could really happen.

A few weeks went by, and then Tom e-mailed me again, asking me if I could testify in front of the Nevada's legislation session to tell my story. Going in front of a legislation committee was pretty intimating and I wished I was more prepared but this was my first time. The people up on the podium were very nice and even though I knew they did not understand everything I said, I think they got the just of it. There were more people that wanted to get the signature stamp bill passed, more than I thought. The only people who opposed the bill were the banks. They were worried about the stamp being stolen. We told the Nevada legislation how guarded we are with our signature stamps and how the person using the signature stamp always needed to be present showing their ID when the stamp was being used. I personally consider my signature stamp as one of my daily essentials that I always keep in my purse, just like my wallet or my medication.

After two years of negotiating with the banks and the legislation, Senate Bill 23 was passed and on May 10, 2005, Governor Kenny Guinn signed my idea into law.

It just goes to show that one person CAN make a difference, even someone like me!

Now, my mark, my signature stamp does mark the spot!

Dear Un-Typical Child

WELCOME TO YOUR WORLD! I want to say that you are beautiful and the world is a better place because you are here. Your parents were so excited to meet you. When they announced that you were coming, they couldn't contain their joy, but now it's not so joyous, because they just found out that you have a disability. They are scared of the unknown and they don't know what the future holds for you. There will be so many questions and not enough answers. You will need to endure a lifetime of evaluations, tests, screenings, meetings, discussions, diagnoses, waiting lists, technology, and so much more. Everyone will want to put a label on you.

Your parents will probably seek help, which they should, but I hope that these supports can see your value in this world and not only your disability. I hope they can see opportunity and not put you into a box, which you can't ever get out of. When the time comes, I hope you go to a typical school, where your friends come from all walks of life. Your friends can make your disability disappear, because they can only see YOU!

Your teachers will teach you what they need to in your own unique way of learning. I hope they push you, so that you know that you have great potential in becoming whoever you want to be. I hope you have inclusive experiences in the real world, so that, when you graduate, you will go into competitive, integrated employment and not ever step into a place where they don't pay you your worth. If you need assistive technology, don't be afraid of it. Embrace it, and make it you own powerful tool.

I need to tell you that your life will not be easy. Society will typically see you as charity, needing help, or being less than others who don't have disabilities. They won't see your gifts and talents and how much you can and will give to society and your communities. You need to teach others that you can advocate for yourself, to take a stance and defend your own convictions, to ask for support, but not to be influenced by their own opinions.

When you are an adult, I hope you do not have to take the paths of our ancestors, you do not have to be segregated working for less than your counterparts, because you have the skills, assisted technologies and confidence that you need to succeed in the real world. I hope you find love and, if you wish, have a family of your own.

Your life will not be easy, no one's life ever is! But I have great hope in you. You have the power to make this world better, more inclusive.

Don't let them negate your humanity for your disability...................

And a new advocate is born!!!!!

I would like to give a special thanks to Robbin Dunn and Stella Meneses for editing this book. Many, many thanks.

www.ingramcontent.com/pod-product-compliance
Lightning Source LLC
Chambersburg PA
CBHW050040080526
44586CB00014B/1386